Selling School Budgets
In Hard Times

by
William Goldstein

Library of Congress Catalog Card Number 84-61201
ISBN 0-87367-215-1
Copyright ©1984 by the Phi Delta Kappa Educational Foundation
Bloomington, Indiana

Table of Contents

Money and the National Mood 7

A Recipe for Receptiveness 10

Showing Is Persuading 13
   Components of the Budget Document 16

Answering Questions Before They Are Asked 18

How Good Is That Budget in the Window? 34

Conclusion 37

Money and the National Mood

Recently a blue-ribbon panel of financial and managerial experts reported that the federal government annually collects more than $280 billion in personal income taxes alone; it also reported that the federal government spends 101% of that paying off its debts for that year before the taxpayer has purchased one micro-moment of *current* government — an astounding and terrifying bit of economic information. In my own state of Connecticut, the State Department of Education has made enormous fiscal errors in the handling of grants (state aid) and reimbursements for school building programs amounting to ten million dollars or more. Across the country a pervasive attitude has developed that those charged with delivering government services are not even coming close to providing a dollar's worth of goods and services for every 100 cents of required tribute.

Confidence in the manner in which public institutions, including our schools, spend their allotted funds is at a low ebb. Charges of waste, fraud, and administrative incompetence exacerbate the anger the American people take to the voting polls, in letters to editors, and in fulminations at social gatherings. The national mood about taxation is one of exasperation over what the government does and how it does it and over what it spends in *not* getting the job done well enough. Clearly, it is not a pleasant climate for school people!

As the schools struggle for their fair share of diminishing tax resources, we are witnessing a form of political cannibalism, with each agency "devouring" another for its cut of the tax dollar. With little consideration given to the relative worth of institutions, the debate has sunk to the level of divisive combat over how the tax pie should be proportionally sliced. And emotional appeals (a form of public begging by stalwart supporters and coalitions on which all causes usually rely) no longer seem to work.

Schools have been told that they will have "to do more with less," that we are in an "age of scarcity," and that the low-quality job they are doing has made us "a nation at risk." The tax-paying public may recognize that teachers are the worst paid profession in America and that teachers of mathematics and science are in critically short supply. Maybe the public wants to make things right but fears throwing good money after bad.

It is in just such a climate that communities today grope to secure dollars to educate their children. This fastback proposes no "Open Sesame" to the pocketbooks of America. While generous to a point, this country has never flooded dollars into its schools in support of serious intellectual values, except when the purchase of intellectual mastery translates immediately into high-paying jobs — usually of a "high tech" kind. Funding for our schools can persuasively be presented when two conditions are met:

1. The nation must genuinely be frightened by the brilliance and fierce energy of national competitors (e.g., the Sputnik era of a quarter century ago and the recent challenge of the Japanese "economic miracle").

2. Either economic times must be good at the moment, or hope for and confidence in better times must lie, as Herbert Hoover once said, "just around the corner."

Fortunately, both conditions exist currently, although it is anybody's guess how long they will persist. Times are still hard, taxes are still high and will get higher. But America is ready to try to "return to those thrilling days of yesteryear," to borrow from the Lone Ranger, and to regain its economic primacy through a renaissance of rigor, standards, and competitiveness in educating its young.

How, then, can citizens be persuaded to open their wallets? That is the mission of this fastback — to present to educators, boards of education and other elected officials, and interested citizens ways of preparing annual school budgets and accompanying fiscal documents to inform taxpayers and, above all, to persuade them to tax themselves *more* in order, in the long run, to have *more*.

This fastback will examine the style, form, and content of the central budget document itself. It will provide an example of a less complicated budget document designed for quick perusal and instant digestion. It will address common questions and how to respond to them. It will discuss the uses of metaphor and other persuasive comparisons associated with school finance so that clarity rather than the tortured lexicon of the accountant becomes the language of explanation, illumination, understanding, and consensus.

There exist no talismans, no amulets, no magical incantations that will easily separate the American taxpayer from his hard-earned, increasingly scarce dollars. Only through the power of irresistible logic, which shows how sound value results from each dollar spent, can the taxpayer be persuaded to provide enough money for the American public school to fulfill its "great expectations."

A Recipe for Receptiveness

Making a plan for spending millions of taxpayer dollars and getting sufficient appropriations to do the job right requires meticulous planning and, when done well, is a skillful psychological weaving of dollars and dreams. This is no easy task because dreams almost always exceed dollars. A recent survey in Nebraska (*Education Week*, 31 August 1983, p. 2) showed clearly that while people realized the need for and, in fact, wanted to raise salaries of teachers in their state, they were unwilling to have their taxes increased locally (of course, additional state aid was acceptable). The point is that all public treasuries are stretched to their limits; and the will to do right, by itself, can no longer carry the day. People need to be convinced that additional taxation will definitely produce additional results, and that what they are buying 1) is being bought by other schools, 2) will provide their children with exactly what they seem to lack, 3) cannot be delivered as economically any other way, or 4) is required by statute or regulation on penalty of withdrawal of state or federal funds for failure to comply with such mandates. The trick is how to apply such arguments with irresistible persuasion.

After years of dealing with the American public, most school administrators would agree that every year at budget time they hear the same questions asked, usually by the same people. Experienced administrators anticipate such questions and are prepared to answer them in a way that is compatible with the political climate of their communities. Budget makers for public schools should be guided by the following considerations in communicating about and presenting proposed budgets:

1. The general public is not constituted of accountants and has little tolerance for petty fiscal detail, even though a few will literally hunt for errors in order to discredit the whole budgetary process.

2. Almost no one in a community, with the possible exception of elected officials, will study and master the central content of the always-lengthy and detailed major budget document. To assume that people will be completely familiar with what budget makers have developed is self-deceiving and illusory.

3. Budgets and deliberations about them are boring to almost everyone. Those who prepare budgets must assume (however cynically) that whatever interest people show in the document results from the central desire to *save money* — not customarily to exercise the generosity of their social consciences.

4. A public well-informed about the instructional program, its potential benefits for students, and its modest costs will be far more hospitable to productive public discourse about increased spending and resulting taxation than one that has had information withheld. In other words, masking, distorting, or perfuming the need for more dollars usually boomerangs in ways that are assuredly counterproductive.

5. Materials used in presenting the budget must be thorough and attractive, but brief. The key to a sound presentation of the budget rests in compressing complicated plans involving large sums of money into an easily digestible format.

6. People understand and remember what they see far better than what they hear. The budget document needs to be augmented by other material — illuminating graphics or handouts brimming with simple-to-understand, pertinent information. Remember: complexity leads to confusion; confusion leads to resentment and bitterness; and lingering bitterness makes losers of us all.

7. Threatening the elimination of successful and popular programs as a ploy to ward off reductions in proposed budgets is a discredited tactic, especially if, as is often the case, such program cuts do not come about. Budget makers have cried "Wolf!" too many times now, and the public has seen only cuddly puppies, not ravaging predators.

8. Organize supportive groups in every school in the district to be present at all public meetings concerned with school needs and proposed spending. Principals should be responsible, along with their P.T.A./P.T.O constituencies, for producing lists of parents and other involved citizens who will "show" when support for the proposed budget is vital. Getting support for a proposed budget translates exactly into "getting the vote out" — and numbers frequently determine the final results.

9. Developing the proposed budget so that it shows a breakdown by individual schools guarantees grassroots participation and involvement of those directly affected. Points to be made about budget items are best driven home *at home* — not at remote all-district gatherings. Principals and P.T.O. presidents are passionate salespersons for *their* children; they are merely supportive when dealing with the children of others.

10. Use media wisely. School authorities should never threaten or plead in the media. The one raises the spectre of intimidation, which invites resentment; the other signals weakness and paints images of a Gulliver lashed helplessly on the shores of Lilliput, feeding television and the press with the emotional grist on which they feed so well.

11. Maintain a controlled stance when presenting the budget. When discussing possible consequences of various budget decisions, use "if-then" statements in a detached but logical manner. This will heighten your credibility and convey that you have thought through all aspects in the planning of the budget.

The best way to open a safe is knowing the combination; using dynamite may destroy its contents. The 11 guidelines suggested above are a "combination" that has worked in selling school budgets. The next section deals with the budget document itself and how it can be used for getting schools the dollars they require.

Showing Is Persuading

About a quarter century ago, Vance Packard became famous when he wrote *The Hidden Persuaders*, in which he exposed the tactics used by advertisers to persuade gullible consumers to buy a product. Today, budget makers are well advised to ignore his revelations. Increasingly, in both public and private sectors, "truth in lending," "right to know," and "sunshine law" mentalities have replaced the razzle-dazzle and slick subliminalism of the "hidden persuaders." Today, especially after the debacle at the Watergate, leaders in the public sector must reveal not camouflage, clarify not confuse.

What, then, can school people and their supporters do to demonstrate the necessity of dollars requested? Schools do not have sales forces as such. Unlike profit-making organizations, school systems are insufficiently funded to be funded well. Nevertheless, "selling" budgets requires informative materials in attractive formats that are convincing to taxpayers. Following are 15 suggestions to consider when presenting a proposed budget.

1. Convince with facts and figures that the system offers a dollar's worth of education for every dollar expended. Convey the view that education is an *investment* rather than an *expenditure*.

2. Use every opportunity to meet citizens directly. But for some, the only means of contact will be through newsletters, flyers, etc.

3. Prepare enough material for meetings no longer than one to one-and-a-half hours. You waste your time when you exceed the listening tolerance of your audience. More is not necessarily better!

4. Always encourage questions. This conveys an open atmosphere in which participation is welcome.

5. Show as much as you can with visuals, keeping lecturing to a minimum.

6. Do not feed more information than people can ingest and digest at a short meeting; to overinform is as risky as failing to inform adequately.

7. Keep the larger issues up front rather than become entangled in specific items. For example, it is far better to discuss what is involved financially in order to get students to write expository prose well than it is to let a word processor for the central office become the focal point for discussion.

8. Use dramatic comparisons to make a point. For example, indicate that the public spends more than $13,000 per year to incarcerate a criminal and only $2,800 a year (or whatever the local figure is) to educate a child. Such comparisons usually are remembered long after the meeting is over.

9. Involve as many staff or other resource persons as appropriateness and efficiency dictate. A superintendent, droning on alone, can anesthetize a group rather quickly. In addition, if only one person is presenting, he or she bears the brunt of hostility and negative criticism, which commonly occurs in budget meetings. Besides, in many fields, specialists know more and can contribute more to what audiences want and need to know.

10. While it is important to meet any group that requests an explanation of a proposed budget, budget makers should avoid overextending themselves by scheduling too many public meetings.

11. It is better to deal generally with the consequences of insufficient funding than to catalogue specific cuts. For example, stating that there will be a shortage of textbooks, without specifying the exact numbers and the subjects in which these shortages will occur, does the trick. However, when the budget indicates a reduction in the number of teachers, it would be prudent to be more specific. For example, the pupil-teacher ratio will have to be increased.

12. Tell the people who pay the bills what they need to know, not necessarily what you think they want to hear. Sending a "best of all

possible worlds" message could unwittingly play into the hands of disbelieving cynics.

13. Test scores are "in." Use them to your advantage when possible. High achievement scores in academic subjects are the result of solid, craftsmanlike teaching. Let your community know that the much ballyhooed "rising tide of mediocrity" is not present in your schools. Also, above-average test scores give children, their parents, faculty, administration, and community-at-large a sense of pride in soaring above the herd. It also plays well with that singular aspect of our national character — the obsession with being Number One.

14. Try to turn incipient defeats into victories. For example, if your teacher-pupil ratios are low (e.g., 1:12), that's "bad" fiscal news but delightful academic news. No superintendent, board of education, or community is comfortable with the highest per-pupil cost in the state or the best salary schedule in the area. When a system is the highest in expenditures, it paradoxically courts disaster, for many see high costs as reflecting inefficiency or profligate spending. So be prepared to point out specifically what those dollars are buying. For example, high faculty morale is related to good salary schedules, which in turn attract and retain the best qualified teachers. Since well-stocked libraries reflect the intellectual climate of a school system, cite the ratio of books per student as a measure of quality that is well worth the cost. In presenting a budget, school officials must never permit themselves or their boards to apologize for having spent properly what needed to be spent.

15. When attempting to convince people to support a legitimate, even generous, spending plan, always keep in the foreground what schools are supposed to do, which is to educate children and youth. Feeding, transporting, and maintaining buildings and grounds are necessary services, but none of them teaches a child much of anything. When questioned on expenditures for the academic program, point out that, as is the case with colleges and universities, there are three primary measures of quality for an academic place. These are: the quality of its faculty, the quality of its library, and the eminence of its graduates. Put these criteria in the limelight when discussing school quality.

Components of the Budget Document

People enjoy being surprised, and the printed budget should be just that — pleasantly surprising by containing answers to almost all questions people could ask. As much as possible, the budget document should be self-explanatory. I would suggest that no budget document is complete without the following information in crisp, uncluttered prose, using graphics and easily understood tables.

- An introductory message from the system's chief school official that summarizes the purpose and costs of the entire operation.
- A set of assumptions that have guided the development of the spending plan, for example, that the rate of inflation as measured by the Consumer Price Index will increase by 2% from that of the past 12 months, or that the population of the district will stabilize at approximately 4,000 students after one more year of 1% to 2% decline. Such assumptions should be classified into three categories relating to: 1) instructional program, 2) administration, and 3) building operations.
- Sources of revenue clearly and accurately portrayed.
- Enrollment histories and projections.
- Data on professional staffing.
- Average class sizes by school building or by level of schooling.
- Division of educational dollars by program for current year, preceding year, and projected year.
- Major sources of change indicated by comparing current year budget with proposed budget.
- Comparison(s) of increases received by the schools with those received by town or city governmental services by percent per year for previous five years. (Taking the time to collect and report data can be both revealing and rewarding.)
- Comparison of costs per pupil with those for surrounding communities or with state or national averages.
- Comparative information on wealth of the community by per capita or per family income (available from census data).
- Recommended new programs and their estimated costs for the proposed budget year.

- Anticipated pupil-teacher ratios districtwide and by separate schools. (This provides one measure of educational equity within the system — an important legal as well as moral item.)
- Instructional and managerial objectives for the coming year stated in plain English.
- Brief commentary on every program to which dollars are attached — what it proposes to do for students and why it is important to preserve or introduce.
- Clear fiscal summaries by program.

The public today is not generous in allowing itself to be taxed for schools for three overriding reasons: 1) it has marginal confidence in what the schools say they can do and even less in what it perceives them as doing; 2) it has never been in the American grain to support intellectual pursuits with unbridled largesse; and 3) it really cannot afford to tax itself much beyond current levels, given the nature of today's precipitous economy. Nevertheless, if taxpayers are given a straightforward and lucid budget presentation that shows precisely how their money is to be spent, you will improve your chances of convincing them to do what they feel is the "right thing" for a tomorrow about which they may be uncertain but in which they definitely have a stake.

Answering Questions Before They Are Asked

If people ask questions (and they should), they are entitled to answers that are brief, accurate, and to the point. Busy people like digests; they relate well to compression but have little patience with pious rhetoric or pompous gibberish such as "enhancing learning environments." When it comes to budgets, people want information — fast, pertinent, honest, and accurate!

Many questions asked about the budget are perennial ones. They can be anticipated and answered before they are asked in what I call a "bird's eye" budget — a small, handy document that is easy to produce, easy to read, and, above all, easy to understand. Preparing such a document is no small task; it requires extracting information from the voluminous formal budget document and using the pertinent facts and figures that will justify the dollars requested.

Although intended for mass distribution, the bird's eye budget can be produced inexpensively in the form of a booklet printed on 8½" x 11" paper, folded and stapled at the middle. Pages might be different colors to separate sections of the document and to make it more attractive. A student-designed cover with symbols appropriate to an educational theme will give the booklet a professional look.

Contents of the bird's eye budget should include:

1. Title page
2. List of the board of education members
3. Brief message from the chief school officer explaining the purpose of the document

4. Well-organized explanations analyzing the budget request for the ensuing year, along with all pertinent data
5. Calendar of scheduled public meetings for deliberations on the budget

To provide more than the above information in a document of this sort tends to overwhelm the reader, and it probably will not be read, thus negating its central purpose as a communication tool.

In my experience the question-and-answer format is the best one to use to answer commonly asked questions. Following is a format used in my own school system in Rocky Hill, Connecticut. The reader should note: the heavy reliance on available data and the use of explanatory footnotes to cross-reference information, the variations in typeface for emphasis, the simplicity of tables, the assumptions that are woven into many of the responses, the absence of any threats to cut or eliminate key programs or personnel, and the sometimes straightforward revelation of less-than-flattering information in order to allow a community to see things as they really are.

Obviously, the kinds of questions and answers will vary in different communities. My purpose is to suggest a possible format for the kinds of questions to which people expect answers and some ways of answering those questions.

Bird's Eye Budget 1983-84
Rocky Hill Public Schools

Q. What was the total budget for this year (1982-83)?
A. $6,016,560

Q. Those dollars represent an increase of what percent over the previous year?
A. 7.1% more than what was appropriated for 1981-82.

Q. What has been the relationship of inflation to increases in appropriation to the schools over the past four years?

A.

Year	Estimated Inflation Rate at Budget Development Time	Increase in Appropriations to Schools
1979-80	9.5%	7.5%
1980-81	14.0%	12.8%
1981-82	12.6%	7.98%
1982-83	11.0%	7.1%

As you can see, the appropriation increases granted the schools have been dramatically less than the rate of inflation, notwithstanding the fact that our student enrollment has declined slightly in each of these years.

Q. What were the enrollments in the Rocky Hill Public Schools at the close of the school year 1981-82 and what are they now?

A.

June 1982	December 1982	% Decrease
1,978	1,915	3.2%

These data show that our population continues to decline, which, in general, is the condition of enrollments throughout the state. You should be aware, however, that we have and are continuing to compensate for that decline by a nearly corresponding reduction in staff.

Q. If the town is growing (and it is), why are enrollments declining?

A. There is no single reason. As everyone knows, young married couples are postponing having families; and, in some earlier instances, certain housing complexes did not permit children. There seems to be no dramatic increase in enrollments in private schools, so we are not losing students to them. In essence, there really is no precise, uncomplicated answer for that question.

Q. If enrollment is declining, are we reducing our staff also?
A. Yes, we are. Our recommended budget this year calls for a net reduction of two teachers. Since 1977-78, our student

population has declined 9.3% and our reduction in staff (if this budget is approved) would be equivalent to a reduction of 8.5% in teachers.

We are recommending the addition of two new teachers — one to reintroduce foreign languages into the junior high school and a music/art combination to be shared among three schools. At the same time, however, we are calling for the reduction of four teaching positions in the district — two in the elementary schools, one in special education, and one at the high school — making a net reduction of two.

Q. Why does the budget continue to escalate at substantial rates when we have fewer children in the schools?

A. Unfortunately, inflation is a fact of our lives — currently at 5%. Consequently, every dollar budgeted is worth 5% less.

Mandates in the form of state and federal requirements continue unabated, despite predictions to the contrary. This past year there has been a sharp reduction in state and federal dollars available for mandated programs, so it is largely the local tax dollar that pays for carrying out these mandates.

In addition, while oil prices have stabilized, there is the threat of dramatic escalation in natural gas prices, and most predictions are for increases of about 20%. Utility costs, as you know from your home bills, have continued to climb, as have the costs for gas.

Negotiated contracts (approximately ¾ of the costs of running the public schools are in employee salaries and benefits) have a dramatic effect on this year's budget and will continue to do so for the foreseeable future. In fact, approximately ½ our recommended increase for 1983-84 is the result of the newly negotiated agreement with the Rocky Hill Teachers Association.

Q. Have we kept pace with other school systems during the past few years?

A. Yes and no. Our school plants are among the best in the state; and our new high school, of course, is outstanding. Our test scores, in general, are very good. We pay our bills on time and do not incur deficits at year's end. However, our salary schedules have been conspicuously lower than those in most communities and have tended to make us uncompetitive with surrounding school systems for teachers in fields where candidates are scarce (e.g., science, mathematics, industrial arts, etc.). We continue to delay purchase of certain equipment such as film projectors and duplicating machines since we do not have excess dollars for adding or replacing such equipment.

Q. What about professional staffing when compared to the rest of Connecticut?

A. For 1981-82, the statewide ratio of pupils to professional staff was 14.2:1, a slight drop from the previous year of 14.5:1. For 1980-81, Rocky Hill was 13.9:1 and for 1981-82 was 12.9:1 — rather favorable when compared to the state average. Source: "Professional Staff Data for Connecticut Public Schools, 1977-78 thru 1981-82," CPEC (October 1982).

However, if this budget is approved and our enrollment projections hold, then our ratio for 1983-84 would escalate to 14.2:1, reflecting the staff reduction as a result of the decline in student enrollment.

Q. Essentially, what was the Board's charge in preparing a budget for 1983-84?

A. Each year the Board gives the superintendent a "budget charge" (that charge appears on page 4 of the complete budget document). In essence, the charge directs the superintendent to develop a recommended spending plan that maintains the current program without a loss of quality, but with sufficient funds to ensure proper and productive operation of the school system.

Q. From where does the money come to support our schools?
A. Page 11 of the complete budget for 1983-84 presents a detailed set of sources. Basically, monies to support education come from local taxes (by far the largest single source in Connecticut), from the state (mostly in the form of what is known as the "Guaranteed Tax Base"), and some from the federal government.

Q. What is the current mill rate?
A. 42.0 mills

Q. How much revenue will one mill produce, given current assessments and the anticipated grand list, that is, the total taxable wealth of the community?
A. It is currently estimated at $265,000 (as of Dec. 21, 1982), which if this proposed budget is approved, would increase 3.69 mills.

Q. What are our average class sizes?

A.
School	Range	Mean Class Size
Moser (K-2)	15 — 22	18.0
West Hill (K-6)	14 — 29	21.2
Stevens (K-6)	14 — 26	19.7
Griswold (7-8)	5 — 16	17.6
High School (9-12)	3 — 27	17.3

Explanatory notes on these figures appear in the complete budget on page 16.

Q. How does that compare with districts of similar size?

A. Favorably. Although there are school systems with lower class sizes, we in Rocky Hill have always prided ourselves on highly manageable classes and, indeed, have them.

Q. How are educational dollars divided by school for this year and next?

A.

School	1982-83	1983-84
Moser	$ 98,315	117,582
West Hill	649,274	743,347
Stevens	626,539	717,057
Griswold Jr. High	612,548	742,786
High School	1,165,709	1,326,144

Q. What is our cost per pupil (dividing total budget by number of children attending public schools in Rocky Hill for the year 1982-83 as of this past November)?

A. $3,139, which represents an increase of 10.3% from the December 1981 figure in last year's calculations.

Q. Out of 169 cities and towns in Connecticut, where does that place us in comparison with the rest of the state?

A. For 1980-81 (the latest comparative data we have), Rocky Hill's per-pupil expenditure was $2,461 (this figure does not include many expenditures included in the figure of the preceding question), placing Rocky Hill 44th in the state out of 169 cities and towns. (Page 25 of the complete budget document contains all pertinent information.)

Q. When compared to 16 surrounding towns, and to the state as a whole, how does Rocky Hill compare in key financial areas?

A. For 1981-82, according to data from the Connecticut Expenditure Council and the University of Connecticut (see pages 26-27 in the complete budget document), the town's effort in funding its schools (not counting the considerable expenditure in building a new high school) is below average for the 16 surrounding communities. Rocky Hill's percentage of town budget devoted to education ranks 14th out of 17; in per capita (not per pupil) expenditures for public education, it ranked 15th out of 17. Note, however, that although Rocky Hill ranked 14th out of 17, its per capita income was 8th out of 17; and our mill rate ranked 8th in 1982 and our per-pupil cost was 9th or at the median for 1980-81.

For the whole state of Connecticut, Rocky Hill ranked 44th in per-pupil cost for 1980-81 and 50th the year before. It should be pointed out that per capita expenditure in Connecticut for public education averaged $433.36 in 1981-82, but Rocky Hill spent only $385.93, or 10.9% **below the state average**.

Q. Do relatively small systems such as Rocky Hill tend to pay more for educating their youngsters?

A. Yes, they do! Small school systems are less cost effective. Frequently class sizes are smaller, but they could easily accommodate more students per class without affecting educational quality. For example, a class of 15 could just as easily be 20 without increasing costs very much.

Q. Where and why do we have some very small class sizes?

A. Obviously, in certain classes, such as special education, the class sizes are very small and must be. The junior high school also has some small classes because of small facilities (e.g., in industrial arts). Most of the small classes are in the high school in advanced courses in foreign languages and specialized courses such as shorthand where enrollment is limited. Our high school is small, but it offers what a good comprehensive high school should offer. If we are to maintain the variety of curriculum offerings in our high school, then we have no other choice but to have some small classes.

Q. How well do our children do on standardized tests?

A. In general, they do very well, indeed! The most recent results on the Stanford Achievement Tests in grades 2, 4, and 6 were as follows:

- Second-graders who completed the achievement battery scored 1.1 years **above** grade level with 100% of all students achieving at or above grade.
- Fourth-graders also scored 1.1 years **above** grade level with 93% scoring at or above grade.

- Sixth-graders were 1.7 years **above** grade level with 98% at or above grade.

Results of Stanford Achievement Tests in the junior high school show our students significantly above average in all tests — in the 6th stanine in 1981 and 1982 in total reading and in the 8th stanine in total mathematics for both those years. The complete battery showed our students scoring in the 8th stanine in 1981 and in the 7th stanine in 1982. Very fine results, indeed!

In the Scholastic Aptitude Test (S.A.T.), our students have scored above the national average in both mathematics and verbal ability 10 out of the last 15 years.

Our students have always scored very well in the state's EERA testing program (minimal competency and basic skills proficiency). The current 9th-graders also scored well at Rocky Hill High School in this composite battery. Here is how our students scored compared to the State Level of Expected Performance (SLOEP) in the last two years of testing:

Area	Above SLOEP* 1981**	Above SLOEP* 1982***
Mathematics	93.4%	89.0%
Language Arts	97.8%	95.0%
Writing Sample	98.5%	98.0%
Reading	98.5%	94.7%

*Acceptable level of minimum competence, requiring no remedial work.

93.3% of our students scored **above the acceptable minimum in all four tests.

***83.2% of our students scored **above** SLOEP on all four tests, and 93.9% scored **above** SLOEP on at least three of the four tests.

As one can see, the dollars expended on the public schools in Rocky Hill achieved substantial academic results.

Q. What part of this year's budget is discretionary, that is, over which the Board and administration have some freedom to spend or not spend?

A. Only 2.88% of the budget recommended for 1983-84 is discretionary. The previous year's budget contained only 3.67% discretionary dollars. This represents a reduction of 21.5% in discretionary dollars. All other expenditures are essentially committed by internal program requirements or outside mandate. Obviously, to cut drastically into personnel or program would be highly undesirable and should be considered only as a last resort for reducing expenditures.

Q. What percent of the budget goes to salaries and fringe benefits?

A. For the current year (1982-83), 75.5%. If the recommended budget is approved, that figure decreases to 74.5%.

Q. Do we pay for the education of children who live in Rocky Hill but attend school elsewhere?

A. Yes, in some instances. The primary example is where special education placement is required either on a daily or residential basis by statute. In addition, we pay tuition for students who attend a state vocational agriculture center at a nearby high school. Students, however, who attend vocational technical schools do so at the expense of the state, although we pay transportation costs.

Q. In the last six years (beginning with 1977), how do percentage increases in additional dollars in the town budget compare with that of the schools?

A.

Year	Percent of Change Town	Percent of Change Schools
1977-78	+ 5.7	+ 7.6
1978-79	+23.8	+10.1
1979-80	+ 3.7	+ 7.5
1980-81	+29.7*	+12.8

    1981-82   + 18.1*   + 7.98
    1982-83   + 14.9*   + 7.1
*includes financing of new high school plant

Q. What is the current annual rate of inflation?
A. Approximately 5% (anticipated to hold through 1984).

Q. Where does the inflation rate have the most conspicuous impact?
A. Dollars for heat, utilities, salaries, supplies and materials, transportation, and out-of-district placement of students in special education. There are other areas, too, but these are the main ones.

Q. If costs of energy and utilities keep rising, what have we done to effect savings in these areas?
A. To keep energy costs down, we have done the following:

- Stevens School: Installed gas/oil combination burners and computerized energy management system.
- Jr. High School: Installed gas/oil combination burners and insulated north end of building.
- West Hill School: Installed computerized energy management system.
- Administration Building: Installed storm windows, lowered ceilings, and added pneumatic control system.
- Moser School: Lowered ceilings.

Ultimately the cost of such systems are self-liquidating as a result of the large savings that would have been expended — in fact, wasted — were it not for these systems.

Q. What is a mandate and who pays for complying with it?
A. A mandate is a requirement established by either the state or federal government for a local school district to do something by way of educating the general student body or a special group of young people. In the long run, you, the taxpayer, fund that requirement and frequently do so out of the

local property tax when the mandate is given without supporting state or federal funds, as is all too often the case.

Q. With these so-called mandates, if there is insufficient or no funding to support what the state or federal government requires local school systems to do, is there any hope of either getting more support or fewer requirements, or both?

A. Past experience indicates that there is little hope of either reducing current mandates or of additional funding for them. Even though it is the policy of the current administration in Washington to reduce regulations in all federal agencies, and it has been successful to some degree, the local schools have been affected very little, at least to this point. On the other hand, with reduction of Chapter I funding (formerly Title I), it has been necessary to augment federal funding by local dollars in order to preserve certain programs for this year.

Q. Special education is costly. Why is this so?

A. Class sizes are very small in most instances. Transportation costs are high and getting higher because of special vehicles needed. Costs for out-of-district placements, either daily or residential, are very high and getting much higher. We have made extra efforts this year to keep special education program costs as low as possible, balancing mandate, cost, and conscience.

Q. All budgets have "fat." Where is ours?

A. The increase this year in our budget is significant; about that there is no doubt. Nonetheless, that increase is essentially beyond our control since approximately ½ of the increase is a result of the negotiated settlement with the Rocky Hill Teachers Association, which when adding 5% inflation to it accounts for some 13% of the 16% increase. Other increases are for contracts with other employees and for huge increases in medical insurance premiums, both of which are beyond our control.

Q. What is the recommended budget for 1983-84 and what percent increase does that represent over the current year?
A. $6,994,779 — an increase of 16.3% over the current year's budget.

Q. Assuming that this budget were to be approved intact, what would the per-pupil cost be, based on enrollment projections?
A. We are projecting an enrollment of 1,910 children. With a budget of $6,994,779, the per-pupil cost for next year would be $3,662. (I would point out that the annual cost of keeping one prisoner in jail is in excess of $12,000.)

Q. What promise is there for stabilizing costs in the near future?
A. The next three years, with inflation in check (5% as compared to 14%), yields the possibility of some reasonable control on increases, especially if enrollment continues to decline. On the other hand, keeping teacher salaries and benefits competitive, with no certainty on energy prices, the possibility of rekindled inflation if interest rates continue to drop and credit eases widely, and the tenuous and declining role of federal and state support in some areas for mandated programs make it difficult to predict what we can do about controlling costs.

In addition, our buildings are one year older and require many more dollars for maintenance. We must negotiate other contracts beyond those with our employees, involving transportation services and maintenance agreements. We do not have much say in legislation requiring us to perform certain functions without adequate funding to execute them. We cannot control the health of our employees or the rapid escalation of insurance premiums. We have very little control over any of these matters, yet we have to fund each and every one of these or else not provide services.

In fact, I suspect the paradox of increased costs with fewer children will plague the public schools for some time to come.

Q. Will Rocky Hill be closing any schools in the foreseeable future?

A. Our current budget calls for five schools and the central office to remain open for 1983-84. We do not foresee closing any school at this time, especially since the Board is committed to keeping Moser School open for at least three more years. However, if we cannot fund all our buildings, then the Board would have to reconsider the number of plants it can keep open, given the budget that it finally receives from Town Council.

Q. What is the status of employee contracts?

A. For 1983-84, all contracts are settled with the exception of certain noncertified individuals and the custodial group. Negotiations for each either has begun or will begin soon.

Q. Just where did our salaries for teachers stand prior to the most recent negotiations with Rocky Hill Teachers Association?

A. Our teachers' salary schedule ranked 26th out of 28 school systems in Hartford county — **very nearly last.** (See page 15 of complete budget document for additional comparative data). A comparison of Rocky Hill with 17 area towns for 1981-82 showed that the mean salary for our teachers was **absolutely last**, nearly $700 below Canton, which was next to the last, and 33.2% below the mean salary in West Hartford, the community with the highest mean salary of those area towns.

Q. If we are forced to lay off teachers because of severe reductions in the proposed budget, how much will the town actually save?

A. Because layoffs will come for the most part from nontenured personnel, most of whom are at or near the bottom of the salary schedule, we used the bachelor's degree at the second-year step on the salary schedule in arriving at net savings. For every teacher we are forced to lay off, we estimate our savings from a low of approximately $10,807 to a high of about $12,080. The community should be aware that we are obligated to pay in the range of approximately $3,600 to $4,400 in unemployment compensation so that "savings" are only about ¾ or less of the cost of a teacher if we are forced into a situation of layoff.

Q. Is the proposed budget for 1983-84 a reasonable one in the light of current circumstances?
A. What is reasonable to one person may not be to another. There is no question that the increase in the proposed budget for 1983-84 is higher than in previous years. The facts are, our children and buildings are here, contracts are negotiated, inflation is what it is, insurance premiums are what they are, and the discretionary monies (2.88% of the total budget), which are not either legally or morally mandated, are the lowest they have ever been.

Substantial reduction in the budget can come only from reduction in program and personnel. In that light, the budget keeps faith with the charge given by the Board of Education, which is to preserve the high quality of public education in Rocky Hill. This budget does that as best it can in the light of current and historical circumstance.

We hope we have anticipated your questions and that you find this brochure informative. We also appreciate everyone taking the time to read it and becoming involved in our deliberations. Thank you so much.

It is important to give some thought to the distribution of the bird's eye budget. Following are some possible outlets: Each child is given one to take home prior to the first public meeting on the proposed budget. Public agencies such as the town hall, libraries, etc., receive copies to pass out to interested persons. Press and other media receive information copies. Copies are available at all budget meetings and regular sessions of the board of education.

Collecting the fiscal and demographic data to produce a bird's eye budget requires a major investment of time in order to do it well. However, that investment will pay handsome dividends in community understanding of the budget process. It not only answers the most commonly asked questions in a direct and simple format but it also will head off any critics who attempt to accuse the school board and administration of inadequate planning or failing to communicate.

How Good Is That Budget in the Window?

Americans no longer accept; they judge! The national paranoia about "padding" budgets has turned out to be not so paranoid in far too many places, starting with our highest level of government. Gross cost overruns by vendors for the military and unquestioned swollen prices for spare parts have become national scandals. Through guilt by association, other public agency budgets also are viewed as suspect. Now few people have either the time, inclination, or technical skill to act as public watchdogs over the school budget. Nonetheless, the public is rightfully indignant when it suspects that there is "fat" in requested appropriations, especially when reductions in prior years failed to yield the dire consequences predicted by school administrators. And frequently the public is unaware that sound management can yield extra dollars at the end of the fiscal year because of tight controls and absolute fidelity to the intent of the original appropriation.

In the last analysis credibility occurs when there is trust in strong leadership with a proven history of things occurring the way leaders said they would — time and again. The budget document, if well executed, can be a powerful instrument for building public confidence. The document strengthens the credibility of school leaders when it ventilates the budget-making process and communicates openly the budgetary thinking of those who developed it. It can allay suspicion and may even yield unanticipated public generosity.

How good is your budget? The following checklist is offered as a way to assess your budget document. It makes no pretense at exhaustiveness; but it does show whether you have dealt with the central issues, answered *common* questions, made required comparisons, and explained what needs explanation.

Checklist for Assessing the Annual School Budget

		Yes	No
1.	Is the proposed budget carefully organized?	( )	( )
2.	Is the document attractive, but inexpensively printed?	( )	( )
3.	Is there a budget charge from the board of education to its administration that sets the philosophical direction for the schools and states the limits on what it deems affordable?	( )	( )
4.	Has the chief school official succinctly summarized the status of the school system, giving reasons for the major areas of increases in spending, and reasons for the elimination of programs that can no longer be sustained, as well as putting forth powerful arguments for needing every dollar requested?	( )	( )
5.	Can one locate information quickly by using the Table of Contents?	( )	( )
6.	Is there a crisply articulated set of assumptions near the beginning of the budget upon which all fiscal planning was built?	( )	( )
7.	Do charts and graphs present complex data for easy comprehension by laypersons?	( )	( )
8.	Does the proposed budget supply information on national economic indicators such as current rate of inflation, shrinkage in federal support for education, and the like — all of which have distinct bearing on dollars needed to maintain or improve programs?	( )	( )
9.	Are anticipated revenues from sources other than local taxation (e.g., state and federal		

aid, grants, etc.) clearly and accurately indicated? ( ) ( )
10. Is there easily understood information on the community's ability to pay for the kinds of school it wants (e.g., tax mill rate, grand list, assessment ratio, etc.)? ( ) ( )
11. Are there ample comparisons of budgets of public agencies in the local community and school districts in surrounding similar communities? ( ) ( )
12. Are there sufficient regional and national comparative data so that citizens are given a broader perspective than just a local one? ( ) ( )
13. Are there pertinent data on enrollments, comparisons to previous years, and intelligent projections for the near future? ( ) ( )
14. Are costs of programs shown clearly, along with other statistical ways of comparing "apples to apples" (e.g., cost per pupil by level of schooling)? ( ) ( )
15. Are comparative data featured on how well students in the school system achieve on standardized tests? ( ) ( )

Checklists have their limitations, but if your responses are littered with "No's", then you might well question the quality of your budget preparation. Any document that attempts to extract millions of dollars from an often reluctant public needs, at the very least, to be procedurally, arithmetically, and philosophically unassailable.